SPOTLIGHT ON EXPLORERS AND COLONIZATION™

VASCO NÚÑEZ DE BALBOA

First European to Reach the Pacific Ocean from the New World

RYAN NAGELHOUT

Rosen
PUBLISHING®

New York

Published in 2017 by The Rosen Publishing Group, Inc.
29 East 21st Street, New York, NY 10010

First Edition

Library of Congress Cataloging-in-Publication Data

Names: Nagelhout, Ryan, author.
Title: Vasco Núñez de Balboa : first European to reach the Pacific Ocean from the New World / Ryan Nagelhout.
Description: New York : Rosen Publishing, [2017] | Series: Spotlight on explorers and colonization | Includes bibliographical references and index.
Identifiers: LCCN 2016002006 | ISBN 9781477788301 (library bound) | ISBN 9781477788288 (pbk.) | ISBN 9781477788295 (6-pack)
Subjects: LCSH: Balboa, Vasco Núñez de, 1475–1519—Juvenile literature. | Explorers—America—Biography—Juvenile literature. | Explorers—Spain—Biography—Juvenile literature. | America—Discovery and exploration—Spanish—Juvenile literature. | Pacific Ocean—Discovery and exploration—Spanish—Juvenile literature.
Classification: LCC E125.B2 N36 2016 | DDC 910.92—dc23
LC record available at http://lccn.loc.gov/2016002006

Manufactured in the United States of America

CONTENTS

THE AMBITIOUS SPANIARD

The Spanish word *conquistador* is often thought to mean "conqueror." But its Latin root—*conquirere*—means "to search for." These ambitious explorers were popular figures in the fifteenth and sixteenth centuries, gaining fame for sailing west from Europe and into the unknown. Conquistadors searched for new lands and what they hoped would be gold and other riches hidden within.

Vasco Núñez de Balboa was an early Spanish conquistador searching for that same glory. Balboa was born in 1475 in Jerez de los Caballeros, part of a poor

region of Spain called Extremadura. Later, he sailed to the New World to search for new lands, often disrupting and mistreating the native populations already living there. The ambitious Spaniard's daring expeditions in South America found much more than just land. In fact, he was the first European explorer to lay claim to an entire ocean.

TO THE NEW WORLD

Balboa came from a respected family but was very poor. His father, whose name was likely Don Nuño Arias de Balboa, was a knight. Vasco was one of four brothers. At a young age he was sent to work as a page for Don Pedro Portocarrero, a wealthy lord living in the Spanish port city of Moguer.

By 1500, Balboa was an adult and no longer paging. He traveled to the New World with an expedition led by Rodrigo de Bastidas. Balboa worked as an *escudero*, or shield, guarding the expedition party. Departing in 1501, the expedition of fifty or so men explored what is now Colombia in South America. The expedition's two ships—

Bastidas, seen in this modern painting, gave Balboa his first chance to explore the Americas by including him on his 1501 expedition to what is now Colombia.

the *Santa María de Gracia* and the *San Antón*—sank after an infestation of wood-eating worms called shipworms. Stranded in the New World, Balboa settled in the island of Hispaniola—which is now divided between Haiti and the Dominican Republic. He would never return to Europe again.

THE STOWAWAY

Balboa became a farmer near a town called Salvatierra de la Sabana on Hispaniola. He raised hogs and grew crops but began to lose money. By 1509 he was avoiding creditors on the island. With no way of getting out of debt, Balboa plotted his escape. In 1510, Balboa hid in a barrel, which was loaded on a ship set to depart Hispaniola. Legend says he hid with his dog, Leoncico.

The voyage he crashed was led by Martín Fernández de Enciso, who had been commanded by the Spanish government to bring aid to the colony of San Sebastián, on the northern coast of South America. Located on the east coast of the Gulf of

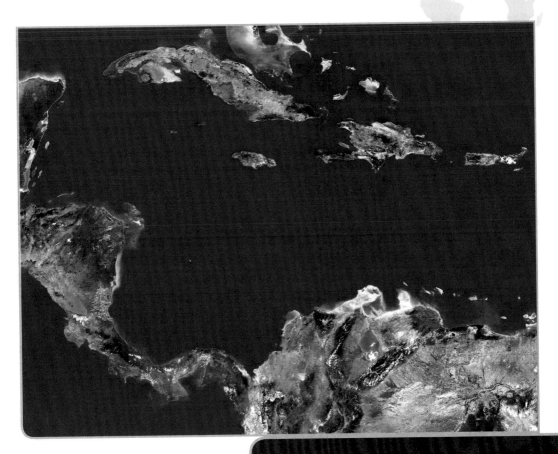

This satellite image shows the Caribbean Sea and the lands and islands surrounding it. Hispaniola is the second-largest island.

Urabá, San Sebastián was founded by Alonso de Ojeda. Balboa was discovered before they arrived in San Sebastián. Stories say Balboa was nearly abandoned alone on an island by Enciso until Balboa convinced the captain he could be useful because of his past expeditions in the region.

SANTA MARÍA LA ANTIGUA

Enciso's expedition found some settlers near what is now Cartagena, Colombia. But Ojeda, who had left two months earlier for Santo Domingo, was not there. The settlers, led by Francisco Pizarro, said that they had basically abandoned San Sebastián because of poison arrow attacks from the native peoples. They were supposed to wait fifty days for supplies from Ojeda, but he never returned and the survivors sailed off in search of safety. About one hundred settlers had died from drowning, starvation, and attacks from native peoples.

No longer just a stowaway, Balboa could now offer useful advice. He suggested the expedition and San Sebastián's survivors

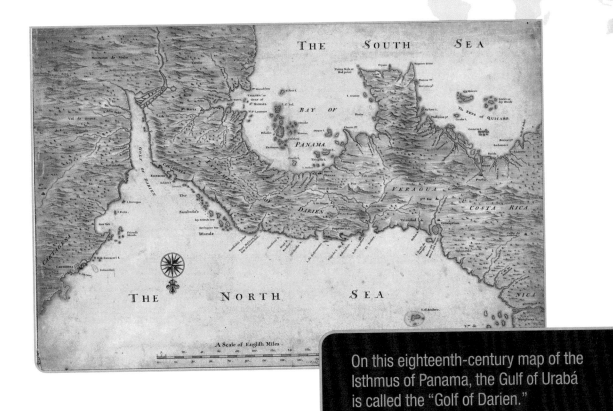

On this eighteenth-century map of the Isthmus of Panama, the Gulf of Urabá is called the "Golf of Darien."

cross the Gulf of Urabá to form a new settlement. He knew the area had good farmland from his expedition with Bastidas. Balboa also said that the native population to the west of San Sebastián was friendlier to outsiders and that they lacked poison arrows. The information helped the Spanish decide where to establish their new settlement, Santa María la Antigua del Darién. The "del Darién" was because the Spanish called the land to west of the Gulf of Urabá "Darién."

GOLD FOR THE CROWN

One of the major reasons conquistadors explored the New World was the chance of finding gold and other riches. The Spanish king, Ferdinand II, said in 1511 "Get gold, humanely if possible, but at all hazards— get gold." Rumors of huge supplies of gold spread among conquistadors, and the explorers also valued pearls, silver, and other precious metals. Bastidas's 1501 expedition, for example, was searching for pearls. But the colony of San Sebastián's primary concern had been finding gold.

As Balboa and the members of the expedition established Santa María, they began trading with native peoples for gold.

At first, Enciso declared he was in charge of Santa María despite the fact that Ojeda's second in command, Pizarro, was still with the settlers. When Enciso threatened to hang anyone found privately trading for gold with natives, the others organized a meeting to set up an official government in Santa María.

Enciso's rules about trading gold made him unpopular with other settlers at Santa María. He essentially took control of all gold

Gold was an important motivating factor in the Spanish colonization of the New World.

trade with the natives. Because of this, when the local government at Santa María was created, Enciso wasn't given any power. Balboa was one of two *alcaldes*

elected. The other alcalde was a man named Benito Palazuelos. The alcades were essentially mayors of Santa María, setting rules and organizing settlers in missions. A man named Bartolomé Hurtado was named the *alguacil*, or sheriff.

Enciso was furious with the elections, which he said constituted treason. Balboa, however, said that because the group had moved from San Sebastián to Santa María the colony was no longer under Enciso's jurisdiction. In the spring of 1511, Enciso was arrested for a number of crimes in Santa María. Without power or support of the other settlers, Enciso was sent back to Hispaniola.

HUMAN TORTURE

With Enciso removed from power, Balboa took full control of Santa María, declaring himself interim governor and captain general. He began searching for gold with the help of the nearby native people, who were familiar with the geography and features of the area. Often, however, this help was given due to force. Balboa and the Spanish routinely tortured Native Americans for information, often letting dogs attack and kill them if they refused to help.

Balboa's dog, Leoncico, would be sent out to chase down Native Americans by grabbing their arms in his mouth. If the Native American let the dog lead him back to Balboa, he would not attack. If the native

This illustration based on a sixteenth-century engraving shows Balboa ordering dogs to attack a group of Native Americans.

fought the dog's pull, however, Leoncico would kill the native and viciously tear his body apart. Leoncico was feared by natives and respected by Spanish soldiers, some of whom also let their war dogs attack natives simply for entertainment.

SLAVERY AND WAR

Slavery was also accepted by Balboa and his comrades in Santa María. Balboa had a black slave named Nuflo de Olano with him during his expeditions. Balboa often organized expeditions to find and acquire native slaves for the Spanish settlers to force into farming and other tasks. Balboa and other conquistadors trained dogs to acquire a taste for natives and used them to track people down during slave-hunting expeditions.

Not all natives were killed or used as slaves. Balboa and his men often took advantage of wars between tribes to acquire gold and slaves from their rivals. One cacique, or chief, named Chima became an

ally after Balboa and the Spaniards raided his village for food in a region called Careta. At first, Balboa entered the village and Chima said his tribe had not grown much food because they were busy in a war with another tribe, led by a chief named Ponca. Balboa attacked Chima later, but the cacique was released and quickly created an alliance with Balboa.

EXPLORING CARETA

Balboa and Chima became allies and shared information. Balboa even married Chima's daughter, solidifying their friendship further. With Chima's aid, Balboa and his men explored the region of what is now Panama called Careta. In the summer of 1511, Chima led Balboa and his men north to an area called Comogra. The chief there, Comogre, welcomed Balboa and held a feast for the Spanish. Comogre's son Ponquiaco told Balboa that Comogre's gold came from the west, farther west than any conquistador had ventured. He also mentioned a large body of water was on the other side of the Isthmus of Panama.

This hand-colored woodcut shows a native Panamanian village from around the time that Balboa arrived in Central America.

Balboa returned to Santa María eager to organize an expedition west. When he arrived there, he learned the king had officially named him the interim governor and captain general of Darién. He wrote back to Spain asking for one thousand men, supplies to build ships, master shipbuilders, and hundreds of weapons to help them fend off attacks from hostile natives.

THE TURNING TIDE

Balboa's requests for supplies and troops were never answered by the Crown. While waiting for a response he put down a potential rebellion in Santa María. He also foiled a plot by hostile natives to burn the colony to the ground. Balboa soon heard rumors that enemies—including Enciso, who had made it back to Spain—had turned the king against him. Now losing support in Santa María and hearing that someone might come to replace him as the governor of Darién, Balboa quickly made his own plans to explore the sea to the west.

With guides provided by Chima, Balboa sets off on September 1, 1513. He was accompanied by 190 soldiers and a number

Though the Atlantic and Pacific are just a few dozen miles apart, the voyage between them was very difficult.

of slaves. Balboa's expedition sailed to Ponca, the narrowest part of the Isthmus of Panama. Fewer than 50 miles (80 km) of land separate the two oceans here, but the dense jungle, swamps, and mountains between them would prove a tough challenge for the expedition.

Moving through the jungle was slow. It often took days to travel just a few miles through the thick foliage full of insects and

This print is one of many images that dramatize the moment at which Balboa caught his first glimpse of the Pacific Ocean.

Vasco Nunez de Balboa

other animals. Some claimed that Balboa's expedition traveled through jungle so dense that they couldn't see the sky for days. The group also suffered through attacks from hostile natives as they fought their way west. The expedition clashed with a cacique named Quarequá and his followers as they headed for a cordillera, or chain of mountains, on the isthmus. Balboa's men eventually drove Quarequá from his village, and the two sides later made peace.

Balboa's guides took him through vines and foliage to the mountains, where they began to climb. On September 25 or 27—their records claim both dates—a guide pointed Balboa to a peak from which the sea could be seen. Balboa climbed the peak with Leoncico, looked west, and became the first European to spot the Pacific Ocean from the east.

MAR DEL SUR

Balboa called the body of water he spotted the Mar del Sur, which is Spanish for "the South Sea." He climbed down from the peak and picked twenty-six men to accompany him to the water to ceremoniously claim it. Coming to a mile or so of flat sand, he waited until the tide came in and waded into the water. With a picture of the Virgin Mary in his right hand and a sword in his left, Balboa claimed Mar del Sur and all the land that touched it for God and Spain.

Balboa named the area he first encountered the Gulf of San Miguel. The discovery of the sea changed the way that many people thought about exploring the new world. Balboa learned that the water

was salty, and that it rose and fell in tides. That meant the body of water was part of an ocean. It was also a clue that Tierra Firme— as the mainland of Spain's empire in the New World was called in the early years— was its own large landmass, rather than just an extension of Asia.

BACK TO SANTA MARÍA

Balboa's expedition was successful, but he wanted to keep exploring the western part of the isthmus. He heard of a large kingdom to the south—likely the Inca Empire—but lacked the ships needed to further explore Mar del Sur. Nor did he have enough men to search for the empire. Balboa and his men turned back for Santa María and arrived there in January 1514.

While Balboa had been away from the colony for less than six months, word of his treatment of Enciso and another removed leader—Diego de Nicuesa—had reached Spain. Years earlier, Nicuesa had been given a grant by Ferdinand II to govern a colony in

The stories Balboa heard of a kingdom to the south most likely referred to the Inca, who built Machu Picchu, the ruins of which are seen here.

what is now Panama. In 1511, however, Balboa had sent Nicuesa away from Santa María and out to sea. He was never seen again. After Ferdinand found out about these actions, he named Pedro Arias Dávila—also called Pedrarias—the governor of Castilla del Oro, including Darién, in June 1514.

BALBOA AND PEDRARIAS

Pedrarias arrived in Santa María with nineteen ships and around 1,500 men in June 1514. Soon after, a messenger telling of Balboa's sighting and claim of the Mar del Sur reached Spain. Ferdinand was impressed by the story—and the potential for more gold and pearls—and the conquistador was restored to royal favor. Balboa was named *adelantado*, or governor, of the Mar del Sur and two provinces, including Panama. He was, however, still under the jurisdiction of Pedrarias's governorship of Castilla del Oro.

Pedrarias was much older than Balboa. In his youth he had been a skilled soldier who fought against the Portuguese. By 1514, he

This woodcut shows Pedrarias attacking native people on the Isthmus of Panama. Like Balboa, Pedrarias became known for his mistreatment of Native Americans.

had become a white-haired general and administrator. While at first Balboa greeted the new governor warmly, the two men were wary of one another. Balboa thought that Pedrarias would find ways to prevent his exploration of Mar del Sur, while Pedrarias believed Balboa would attempt to replace him as governor of Castilla del Oro.

For a while, Balboa and Pedrarias tried to coexist in Santa María. But the two Spaniards struggled to get along. Pedrarias, for example, was surprised that Balboa's

Balboa discovered the Pearl Islands on the Pacific side of the Isthmus of Panama, but Pedrarias prevented him from exploring them.

dog, Leoncico, was paid the same as human soldiers in Balboa's army. Pedrarias also believed that Balboa's role as adelantado could grow into an independent position of power if he could found a colony elsewhere. Hunger and disease had killed many of Pedrarias's men, and he feared that Balboa—still popular with many in Santa María—would speak against his leadership and damage his reputation.

Santa María's first bishop, Juan de Quevedo, attempted to help the two men make peace. It's written that Pedrarias even betrothed one of his daughters—María, who still lived in Spain—to Balboa by proxy. Still, Balboa grew frustrated by Pedrarias while trying to plan further exploration of the South Sea. Instead, Gaspar de Morales and Francisco Pizarro were allowed to explore the Pearl Islands, which Balboa had discovered in 1513.

EXPLORING THE SOUTH SEA

Finally, in 1517, Balboa made his second trip to explore the Mar del Sur. He was already in the process of gathering ship-building supplies, guns, and food from Cuba when Pedrarias discovered his intentions. Already tied to him through his daughter María's betrothal, however, the governor allowed Balboa to go forward with his plans.

Balboa moved to the western side of the isthmus with his men. For weeks, thousands of slaves carried ship pieces and other equipment more than 50 miles (80 km) through mountains and swamps to a shore south of Adá. There, brigantines were assembled in the Gulf of San Miguel. As construction began on the ships, workers

This woodcut shows Balboa's men cutting timber to replace the wood that had been infested by shipworms, which was a common problem at the time.

noticed the wood they brought over the mountains had been damaged by shipworms. Timber for two new brigantines had to be cut along the Balsa River, but a flood then washed the good timber away.

Exploring new territory helped people create maps of the New World. This map from 1653 shows how the Spanish built on Balboa's discoveries in the following decades.

After multiple delays, the new ships were made and Balboa finally set sail on the Pacific. He made a base on Isla Rica, which means "Rich Island," and took about one hundred men with him to sail south down the mainland for the next year. He sailed toward present-day Peru, sending back to Santa María for more supplies and reinforcements.

While he was away, however, a new governor was set to replace Pedrarias in Santa María. Lope de Sosa, acting governor of the Canary Islands, was on his way to the colony. Balboa heard about this possible change while exploring, and though he feared Pedrarias the news also meant a possible change in his standing in Tierra Firme. Balboa sent a group back to gather information about the change and to see if Sosa had arrived. What he didn't know was that Sosa had died in the harbor before reaching Santa María.

DOWNFALL AND DEATH

Balboa's information-gathering party was discovered by Pedrarias, who then set in motion the final events of Balboa's life. Pedrarias was worried that others had hurt his reputation in Spain, and he feared that Balboa would speak against him if asked. Pedrarias wrote to the conquistador, asking him to return to the colony to discuss matters. When he returned home, Balboa was arrested.

Charging him with high treason, rebellion, and a variety of other crimes, Balboa's judge was Gaspar de Espinosa, a close friend of Pedrarias's. Balboa was quickly found guilty and sentenced to death. Not allowed an appeal, Balboa was beheaded in Santa

Some conquistadors were killed not by natives they conquered, but by other conquistadors. Both Balboa and Pizarro were among those who met this fate.

María on January 12, 1519, along with four others. Santa María was abandoned by the Spanish soon after Balboa died. Natives burned the settlement to the ground in 1524. The place where Balboa spent seven years of his life, where he saw his life end, vanished from the map without a trace.

LASTING LEGACY

Vasco Núñez de Balboa left behind a complicated legacy. The explorer's enthusiastic slave-taking expeditions and use of dogs to torture and kill Native Americans—especially gay men—has tarnished his legacy in the United States and his native Spain. Some historians neglect to mention Balboa among the more famous conquistadors such as Hernán Cortés or Francisco Pizarro. In his "On First Looking into Chapman's Homer" the nineteenth-century English poet John Keats even mistakenly named Cortés as the first European explorer to sight the Pacific Ocean.

In Panama, however, Balboa is still viewed as a hero. The anniversary of his crossing

Balboa has a mixed legacy. He is a hero in Panama, hated by many for his treatment of the Native Americans, and forgotten by others altogether.

the Isthmus of Panama is celebrated with a five-day festival every year. He also appears on coins, and the Panama Canal lock nearest to the Pacific is called the Port of Balboa. More than five hundred years after he claimed the Mar del Sol and all the land it touches for Spain, our views of colonialism and human rights are very different. His accomplishments exploring the Americas on behalf of Spain, though, are undeniable.

GLOSSARY

administrator A person who carries out government business.

ally A person, group, or country working with another toward a common goal.

betrothed Promised to marry or give in marriage.

brigantines Square-rigged ships with two masts but no mainsail.

cacique Native American chieftains in Central America.

ceremoniously In a formal, conscious manner.

creditor A person to whom a debt is owed.

dense Thick or crowded.

expeditions Journeys made for a specific purpose, such as exploration.

foliage A mass of leaves of a plant.

hazards Sources of danger.

humanely With sympathy or consideration for others.

infestation A large group of insects spread out or swarming over an area.

isthmus A narrow strip of land connecting two larger areas of land.

jurisdiction The limits or territory where power may be exercised.

page An assistant or servant who delivers messages.

proxy Power held by one person to act for another.

rebellion An open fight with one's government.

routinely On a regular basis.

treason Betrayal of one's own country or people.

American Embassy Panama
9100 Panama City PL
Washington, DC 20521
(507) 317-5000
Website: http://panama.usembassy.gov/index.html
The land that Balboa explored on his most famous
   expeditions is now part of the country of Panama.
   Americans can contact the American embassy
   there to learn more about the country today.

Gilder Lehrman Institute of American History
49 West 45th Street, 6th floor
New York, NY 10036
(646) 366-9666
Website: https://www.gilderlehrman.org/category/
   coverage-organizations/conquistadors
The Gilder Lehrman Institute of American History is
   a nonprofit organization dedicated to improving
   history education through programs for teachers
   and students. It has received awards from the
   White House, the National Endowment for the
   Humanities, and the Organization of American
   Historians.

Mariners' Museum and Park
100 Museum Drive
Newport News, VA 23606
(757) 596-2222
Website: http://www.marinersmuseum.org

This group of museums holds some of the largest collections of artifacts and historical objects on the exploration of the Western Hemisphere. The museum also maintains a website with information about history's greatest explorers.

National Museum of the American Indian
4th Street and Independence Avenue SW
Washington, DC 20560
(202) 633-1000
Website: http://www.nmai.si.edu
The museum, which also has a branch in New York City, has a diverse collection of artifacts relating to Native American culture. While the museum focuses primarily on the peoples of what is now the United States, it does have materials from Central and South America, too.

Websites

Because of the changing nature of Internet links, Rosen Publishing has developed an online list of websites related to the subject of this book. This site is updated regularly. Please use this link to access the list:

http://www.rosenlinks.com/SEC/balboa

FOR FURTHER READING

Anderson, Michael. *Biographies of the New World: Leif Eriksson, Henry Hudson, Charles Darwin, and More*. New York, NY: Britannica Educational Publishing, 2013.

Bodden, Valerie. *Conquistadors*. Mankato, MN: Creative Paperbacks, 2014.

Cooke, Tim. *The Exploration of South America*. New York, NY: Gareth Stevens Publishing, 2013.

Donohue, Moira Rose. *Vasco Núñez de Balboa*. Hamilton, GA: State Standards Publishing, 2014.

Embacher, Eric. *Stowed Away*. Costa Mesa, CA: Saddleback Educational Publishing, 2013.

Gunderson, Jessica. *Conquistadors: Fearsome Fighters*. Mankato, MN: Creative Education, 2013.

Matthews, Rupert. *Conquistadors*. New York, NY: Gareth Stevens Publishing, 2016.

Mitten, Ellen. *Early Explorers*. North Mankato, MN: Rourke Educational Media, 2014.

Ollhoff, Jim. *The Conquistadors*. Edina, MN: ABDO Publishing, 2012.

Otfinoski, Steven. *Native Americans at the Time of the Explorers*. Pelham, NY: Benchmark Education Company, 2011.

BIBLIOGRAPHY

"Balboa and the Pacific." *Chronicles of America.* Retrieved January 10, 2016 (http://www.chroniclesofamerica.com).

Bernstein, Peter L. *The Power of Gold: The History of an Obsession.* Hoboken, NJ: Wiley and Sons, 2000.

Coren, Stanley. *The Pawprints of History.* New York, NY: Free Press, 2002.

Lidz, Franz. "Following in the Footsteps of Balboa." *Smithsonian.* Retrieved January 10, 2015 (http://www.smithsonianmag.com).

Marcovitz, Hal. *Vasco Nuñez de Balboa.* New York, NY: Chelsea House, 2013.

Markham, Edwin. *The Golden Quest: The Age of Conquest.* New York, NY: William H. Wise & Company, 1909.

Ober, Frederick A. *Vasco Nuñez de Balboa.* New York, NY: Harper and Brothers Publishers, 1906.

Otfinoski, Steven. *Vasco Nuñez de Balboa: Explorer of the Pacific.* Tarrytown, NY: Benchmark Books, 2005.

"Panama." The Word Factbook, CIA. Retrieved January 10, 2016 (https://www.cia.gov).

Thomas, Hugh. *The Slave Trade: The Story of the Atlantic Slave Trade: 1440–1870.* New York, NY: Simon & Schuster, 1997.

"Vasco Nunez de Balboa." Mariner's Museum. Retrieved January 10, 2016 (http://ageofex.marinersmuseum.org).

INDEX

About the Author

Ryan Nagelhout is a children's author and journalist living in Niagara Falls, New York. Ryan graduated from Canisius College in Buffalo with a degree in communications and a minor in classics. He's written about early American exploration and Native American history in a variety of Rosen Publishing titles. Ryan took a keen interest in local history at a young age, researching and writing in the *Niagara Gazette* about influential members of Niagara County to celebrate the county's bicentennial. He enjoys hiking the Niagara Gorge below Niagara Falls and hopes to one day travel to Panama to view for himself the "Southern Sea" Balboa spotted atop the isthmus centuries ago.

Photo Credits